The Flying Football

June Crebbin
Illustrated by Susan Hellard

CAMBRIDGE
UNIVERSITY PRESS

Max liked playing football. Every day he played at school with his friends.

One day, he took a new football to school.

At playtime, Max played football with his friends. But Josie kicked the ball too hard. It landed in the big bin near the kitchen.

"Sorry," said Josie.

Just then, the bell rang. Max said, "You go in, Josie. I won't be long."

Max fetched the caretaker.

"Mr Smith," he said. "My football's gone in the bin."

Mr Smith smiled. "I suppose it flew in all by itself!" he said.

"Can you see it?" asked Max. "It's a new one. It's got my name on."

Mr Smith lifted the football out of the bin. "Here it is," he said. "It's a bit messy."

Mr Smith helped Max to wash the football under the tap.

"There," he said. "It's as good as new. Now keep an eye on that football."

In school, Miss Parker looked round the classroom.

"Where is Max?" she said.

“He’s getting his football,” said Josie.

“And where is his football?” asked Miss Parker.

“In the bin,” said Josie.

Max came in. “Sorry I’m late,” he said.
“My football flew into the bin.”

“That football must have wings!” said Miss Parker.

At lunch-time, Max and his friends had another good game of football. But just as the bell rang, one of the boys kicked the ball too hard.

It flew over the hedge into a garden.
"Oh no!" said Josie.
"You go in," said Max. "I won't be long."

Max fetched Mr Smith.
“And where is it this time?” said Mr Smith.

“In somebody’s garden,” said Max.
Mr Smith got it back again.

But at playtime that afternoon, *Max* kicked the ball too hard. It flew over the fence and landed in a coal lorry that was passing by.

Max went into school feeling very sad.

"What's the matter, Max?" asked Miss Parker.

Max told her.

"Oh dear!" said Miss Parker. "It flew *too* far this time."

Just before home-time, there was a knock at the door. Mr Smith came in.

"Look what I've got," he said.

Max jumped up. “My football!” he said.

“The driver of the coal lorry brought it in,” said Mr Smith. “You’re very lucky.”

"There," said Miss Parker. "I told you that football had wings – and now it's flown right back to you!"

Biffo

COAL
COAL
Cole's Coa
Cole's Coal
Cole's